BE POSITIVE good things are GOING TO HAPPEN

igloobooks

Designed by Simon Parker
Edited by Natalie Graham

Published in 2020
First published in the UK by Igloo Books Ltd
An imprint of Igloo Books Ltd
Cottage Farm, NN6 0BJ, UK
Owned by Bonnier Books
Sveavägen 56, Stockholm, Sweden

Manufactured in China. 1120 002
10 9 8 7 6 5 4 3 2

Library of Congress Cataloging-in-Publication
Data is available upon request.

ISBN 978-1-80022-832-0
IglooBooks.com
bonnierbooks.co.uk

NOTHING IS IMPOSSIBLE.
ONLY IMPROBABLE.

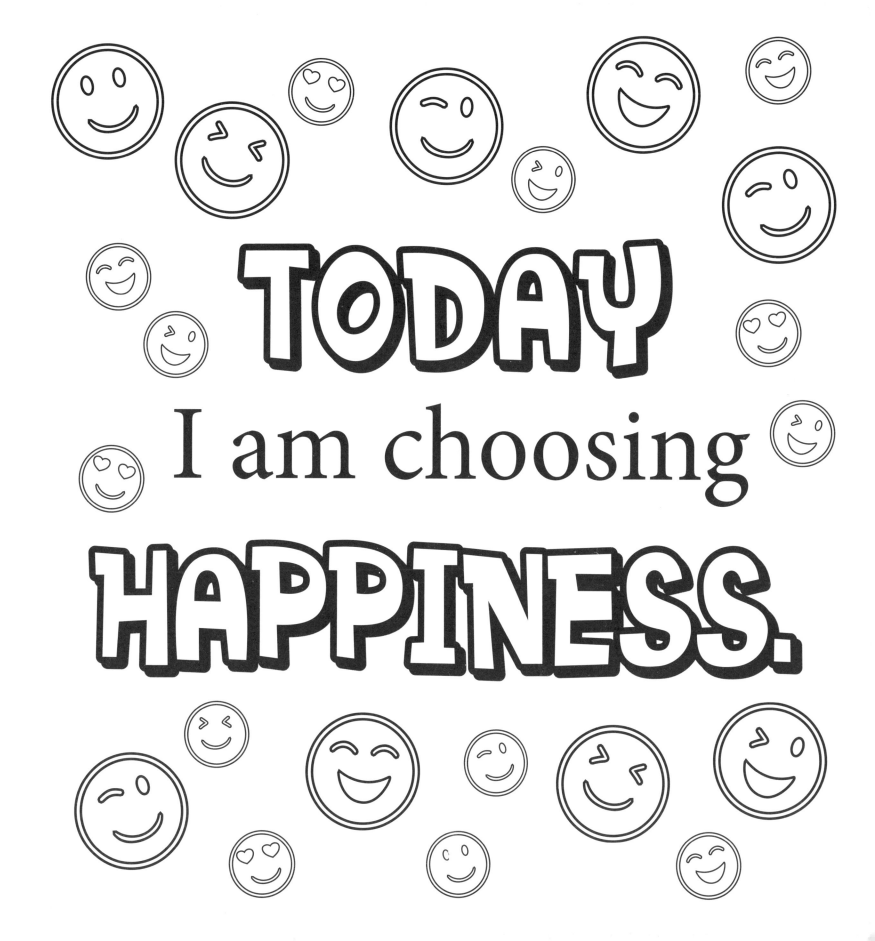

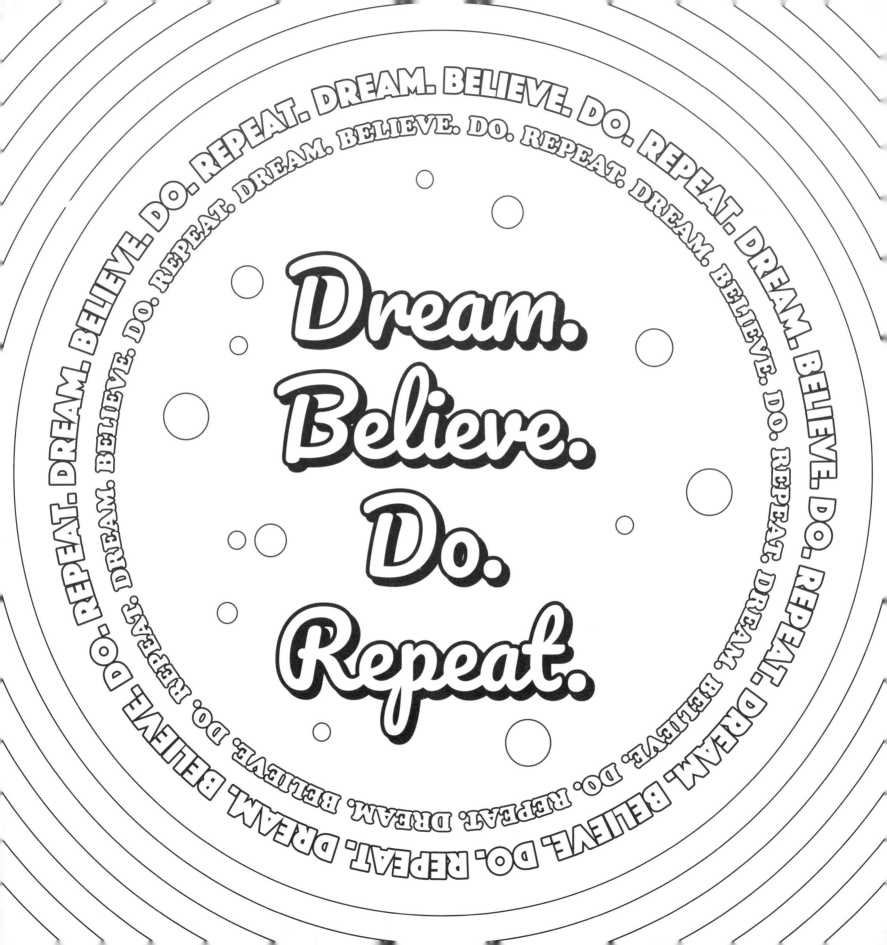

IN PURSUIT OF MAGIC

DIFFICULT ROADS LEAD TO BEAUTIFUL DESTINATIONS.

KEEP SMILING

AND CARRY ON!

The best view comes after the hardest climb.

We age not by years,
but by stories.

Always start your day with a cup of positivitea

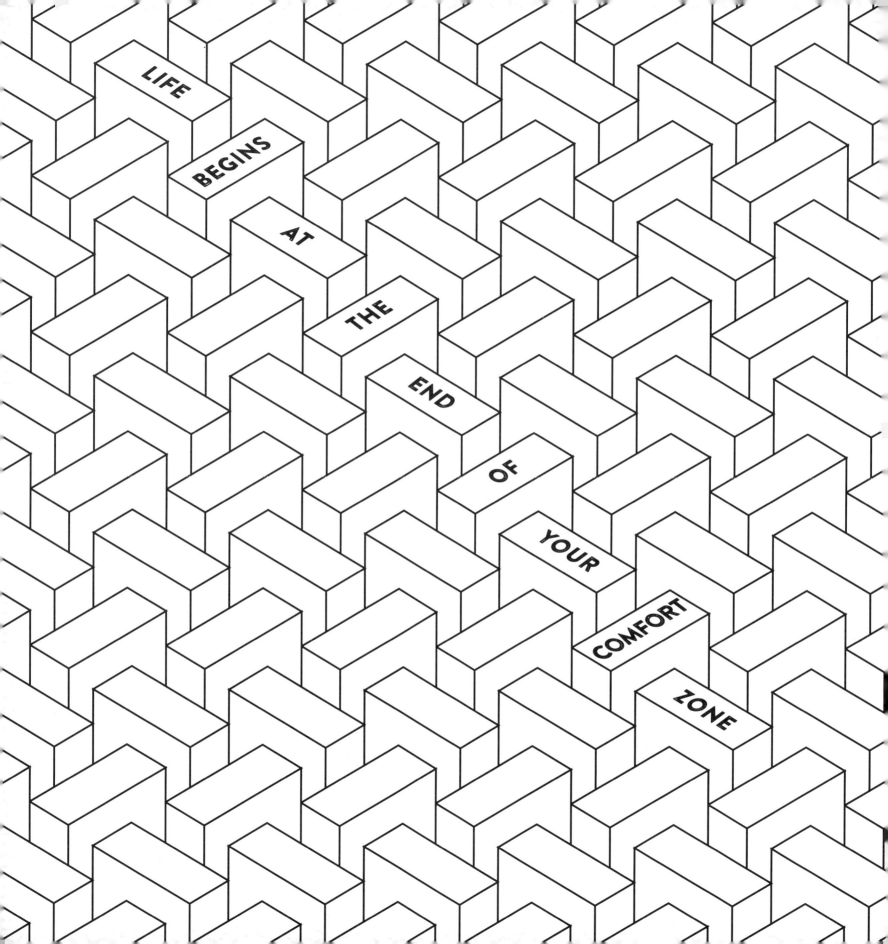

LIFE BEGINS AT THE END OF YOUR COMFORT ZONE

TRUST THE TIMING OF YOUR LIFE

Find the beauty in all that is around.

WORK HARD in silence.
Let SUCCESS make the noise.